Claim the Victory!

Claim the Victory!

The Book of Joshua

This inductive Bible study is designed for individual, small group, or classroom use. A leader's guide with full lesson plans and the answers to the Bible study questions is available from Regular Baptist Press. Order RBP1641 online at www.regularbaptistpress.org, e-mail orders@rbpstore.org, call toll free at 1-800-727-4440, or contact your distributor.

REGULAR BAPTIST PRESS
1300 North Meacham Road
Schaumburg, Illinois 60173-4806

*The King James Version is the English translation used
in our Sunday School curriculum.*

The Doctrinal Basis of Our Curriculum

A more detailed statement with references is available upon request.

- The verbal, plenary inspiration of the Scriptures
- Only one true God
- The Trinity of the Godhead
- The Holy Spirit and His ministry
- The personality of Satan
- The Genesis account of creation
- Original sin and the fall of man
- The virgin birth of Christ
- Salvation through faith in the shed blood of Christ
- The bodily resurrection and priesthood of Christ
- Grace and the new birth
- Justification by faith
- Sanctification of the believer

- The security of the believer
- The church
- The ordinances of the local church: baptism by immersion and the Lord's Supper
- Biblical separation—ecclesiastical and personal
- Obedience to civil government
- The place of Israel
- The pretribulation rapture of the church
- The premillennial return of Christ
- The millennial reign of Christ
- Eternal glory in Heaven for the righteous
- Eternal torment in Hell for the wicked

CLAIM THE VICTORY
Adult Bible Study Book
Vol. 53, No. 4
© 2005
Regular Baptist Press • Schaumburg, Illinois
www.regularbaptistpress.org • 1-800-727-4440
Printed in U.S.A.
All rights reserved
RBP1644 • 0-87227-409-8

Contents

Preface

What a promise God gave Joshua! Every inch of Canaan that his foot stepped on would be his. No ifs, ands, or buts! The promise was ironclad. But claiming the land would not be easy. The Canaanites were trained warriors who would not just roll over and play dead. They would fight furiously. To make matters more challenging, some drove iron chariots.

Joshua knew these facts. Forty years earlier he had joined a delegation of spies in a mission to search Canaan. The group had seen giants and well-fortified cities, but they also discovered that the land was everything God had said it was—lush and productive. Only Joshua and Caleb urged the Israelites to go up at once to possess the land. The other spies predicted disaster if Israel entered Canaan. As is often the case, a faithless majority focused on obstacles, whereas a faithful minority looked beyond the obstacles and saw God's power and faithfulness.

Joshua became Moses' successor and Israel's commander. Braced by God's sweeping promise of success, he was ready to lead Israel into Canaan and claim victory over Israel's foes. He knew the challenge was enormous, but he also knew God's sufficiency was indisputable.

You may be facing enormous challenges: a severe illness, a strong temptation, a hectic work schedule, a family problem, a financial crisis, or a job loss. Will you believe God's promises and claim the victory, knowing that His power and faithfulness are as reliable today as they were when Joshua entered Canaan?

As you explore the book of Joshua, confront with faith every challenge life throws at you. Know that you are more than a conqueror through Christ. Claim the victory!

The Character of a Leader

Joshua 1:1–9

"Have not I commanded thee? Be strong and of a good courage; be not afraid, neither be thou dismayed: for the LORD thy God is with thee whithersoever thou goest" (Joshua 1:9).

An eye-catching bumper sticker advises, "Don't follow me. I'm lost too!" Perhaps many leaders of nations should signal the same message to their followers. The world certainly seems to be following leaders who have no sense of direction while they rush to destruction. Even a segment of the church seems to lack confident leadership. It lacks a clear mission statement and leaders who fearlessly trust God for victory over the enemy and the power to wrest souls from his power. And it needs single-minded men and women of faith who can say to a bewildered world, "Follow me! I will take you to my Leader!"

Getting Started

1. Who do you consider the greatest leader of the last century? What made him or her such a great leader?

2. What challenges do you think every leader must face?

3. Why does a church need strong leaders?

Searching the Scriptures

For forty years Moses had guided the Israelites through the wilderness, transmitted God's laws to them, and borne the full responsibility of their welfare. All history would look back with admiration to this man of God who possessed extraordinary talents of leadership. But Moses had died just when Israel was poised to enter Canaan. How could the Israelites possibly enter and conquer Canaan unless another person with leadership character and skills similar to those of Moses accepted the challenge?

Of course, the Lord had the right person in mind. He spoke to Joshua, saying, "Moses my servant is dead; now therefore arise, go over this Jordan, thou, and all this people, unto the land which I do give to them" (Joshua 1:2).

4. Read Exodus 17:10, Numbers 14:5–9, 27:15–20, 32:12, and Deuteronomy 34:9. Based on these Scriptures, how would you characterize Joshua?

5. Read Deuteronomy 1:38. What had the Lord predicted about Joshua?

Because Joshua had humbly followed the Lord, he had arrived at a high level of spiritual maturity. He knew how to take the shocks and jolts of the journey and maintain his equilibrium. When God allowed trials and difficulties to occur, Joshua simply used them as occasions to move closer to Jehovah and learn lessons that the majority of his countrymen missed. He had heard the murmuring and the complaints of those who had refused to trust God to prove Himself to them. The atmosphere in which he lived was largely one of unbelief. Yet in spite of the Israelites' unbelief and overwhelmingly difficult circumstances, Joshua believed. He had learned by experience that the just must live by faith. The wilderness lay behind him; and just across the river, Canaan opened to receive him and his followers.

The land belonged to Israel because God had given it to them, but their occupation would be contested every mile of the way. Today, too, the enemy contests every effort to claim territory for Christ. Satan, the god of this world, and his cohorts vigorously oppose us. We must "be strong in the Lord, and in the power of his might" (Ephesians 6:10).

Leading Israel in the conquest of Jordan would demand dedication and persistent effort, but the Lord gave Joshua ironclad promises that would encourage him. These promises were both short-range and long-range.

6. What short-range promise did the Lord give Joshua in Joshua 1:3?

7. What long-range promise did he give in Joshua 1:4?

The Promised Land, which God had promised first to Abraham and then to Moses, stretched from the wilderness on the south to the Lebanon mountain range on the north and from the Euphrates River on the east to the Mediterranean on the west. Having scouted part of the Promised Land thirty-eight years earlier, Joshua knew from personal experience that it was a verdant, fruitful land.

8. How does Deuteronomy 8:7–10 describe Canaan?

All who lead God's people must cherish His promises and keep their eyes on the goal He has set. God had given the Israelites a vast and productive land, but Joshua would have to encourage them to take it step by step (Joshua 1:3). Victory was ensured because of the Lord's promises.

9. What did God promise Joshua in Joshua 1:5?

10. What promises has the Lord given you that demand action on your part? (For help, see Psalm 37:4, Matthew 7:5–8, Galatians 6:9, and Philippians 4:6 and 7.)

Joshua had witnessed the Lord's goodness and power in the wilderness. For example, he had seen Him miraculously provide manna, quail, and water (Exodus 16:11–16; 17:5, 6; Numbers 20:7–11), and he had witnessed His mighty power over the fierce Amalekites (Exodus 17:9–13). Still, fresh challenges lay ahead in Canaan. To be an effective leader, Joshua would need to be "strong and of a good courage . . . and very courageous" (Joshua 1:6, 7). Past victories could serve as guideposts, but they were not to be hitching posts.

11. What has the Lord done for you in the past that encourages you to trust Him in the future?

12. Why does a Christian leader never reach a point in life where he or she can coast? (Hint: see Proverbs 16:18 and 1 Corinthians 10:12.)

Joshua's success as a leader would depend in large measure on a proper relationship to God's Word. The Lord commanded him first of all to obey it: "Turn not from it to the right hand or to the left" (Joshua 1:7). Strength of character is essential to leadership. Who would follow a leader into battle if that leader showed no integrity? If a person cannot be trusted to do the right thing, he or she cannot be trusted to guide a nation. By submitting to the authority of God's law, Joshua would be able to say, "Do as I do," not simply, "Do as I say."

13. The apostle Paul understood how important obedience to Scripture is in the life of a leader. What did the Lord, through Paul, command Timothy (1 Timothy 4:16) and Titus (Titus 1:7–9) to do with God's Word?

The Lord commanded Joshua to meditate in the book of the law day and night (Joshua 1:8).

14. a. Why did God insist that Joshua meditate on God's Word? Was he not already a success?

b. Look back at the answers you recorded for question 4. What, if anything, is missing from Joshua's reputation? Which of Joshua's qualities were permanent regardless of what he did in the future?

15. What is the significance of meditating on the Word day and *night?*

16. What hope of success does a Christian leader have if he or she uses the Word for public ministry but does not use it for personal growth?

17. Read Matthew 4:1–11. What weapon did Jesus use to ward off Satan's attacks? _____ Read Joshua 1:8, Psalm 119:9–11, and 2 Timothy 2:15. How can a person become proficient in using this weapon?

Finally the Lord repeated His charge that Joshua be strong and courageous. Neither fear nor dismay were to blunt his leadership (Joshua 1:9). His success was guaranteed, because the Lord, his God, would be with him wherever he went. The promised constant presence of the Lord must have encouraged Joshua later when he crossed the Jordan, marched around the strongly fortified city of Jericho, exercised decisive discipline within his own ranks, and battled well-armed foes.

We Christians may also depend on the Lord's presence. He is with us wherever we go.

18. Read Romans 8:35–37. According to this passage, over what adversities do we triumph through Christ?

We never offer a gospel witness alone, face a trial or temptation alone, or confront a hostile world alone. The Lord is with us "alway, even unto the end of the world" (Matthew 28:20). He pledged, "I will never leave thee, nor forsake thee" (Hebrews 13:5). Like Joshua, we have every good reason to do God's will.

Making It Personal

Those who are involved in full-time, vocational Christian service are not the only ones with leadership responsibilities. Every Christian adult is a leader somewhere. At home as a parent, a mom or dad must lead the children in God's ways. At work a Christian should endeavor to lead his or her associates to know Jesus Christ. How well are we providing godly leadership?

19. a. List the Christian leadership roles you fill.

   b. Evaluate whether you have been successful in each of your Christian leadership roles. Put a plus sign next to each one in which you are growing and succeeding. Put a minus sign next to each one in which you are not growing and not enjoying success.

20. Finish the following two sentences with a brief description of your regular approach to each of these activities:

   I read the Bible . . .

   I meditate on the Word . . .

21. What correlation do you see between the pluses and minuses from your list above and the descriptions you wrote in question 20?

22. What steps will you take to become better acquainted with the
Lord through the Scriptures?

(1)

(2)

(3)

(4)

(5)

Lesson 2

At the End of Her Rope

Joshua 2:1–24

"And as soon as we had heard these things, our hearts did melt, neither did there remain any more courage in any man, because of you: for the LORD your God, he is God in heaven above, and in earth beneath" (Joshua 2:11).

I've reached the end of my rope!" We associate this common saying with jangled nerves and a desperate situation. A mother may be at the end of her rope because her teenage son or daughter seems out of control. A distraught worker may feel he is at the end of his rope when every effort to please the boss fails. A couple with no cash reserves may think they are at the end of their rope when unexpected medical bills pile up. In this lesson, we meet a woman at the end of her rope, but her rope was a lifeline and a guarantee of survival. She was Rahab, a resident of Jericho.

Getting Started

1. As a child, whom or what did you normally turn to for help during a frightening storm?

2. How did your courage increase or decrease according to how closely you sensed the presence of your help?

3. Honestly, how much ability did that person or thing really have to keep you safe?

Searching the Scriptures

Word that the Israelites were coming to Canaan had reached the residents of Jericho, but Rahab had no way of knowing that two of them would visit her in person. The two were messengers, or spies, whom Joshua sent on a reconnaissance mission. Upon reaching Jericho, they entered Rahab's house, but word of their arrival reached the king of Jericho. (See Joshua 2:1 and 2.) He dispatched his men to apprehend Joshua's two messengers, but Rahab had hidden them on the roof under a pile of flax (vv. 3–6).

4. What did Rahab tell the king's messengers about the two spies?

5. Do you think lying to spare human life is ever right (for example, in time of war)? Explain.

6. How did God view Rahab's lies according to Proverbs 12:22?

7. Read Hebrews 11:31. How do you balance Rahab's faith in God with her lies to the king's messengers?

Before sending Joshua's messengers on their way, Rahab told them the people of Jericho were afraid of the Israelites. They knew the Lord had given the Israelites the land of Canaan.

8. According to Joshua 2:10, what two events convinced the people of Jericho and Canaan to fear the Israelites?

9. a. When did the people of Jericho first hear about the Israelites and their deliverance from Egypt (Numbers 14:1–4, 11–16)?

   b. What did they hear about Israel's God (Numbers 14:14)?

   c. How does what they heard compare to the emphasis of God's charge to Joshua according to Joshua 1:9?

10. a. According to Joshua 2:11, what did Rahab say the people of Jericho had lost?

   b. How does this compare to Moses' predictions of what the Red Sea crossing would do to the inhabitants of Canaan (Exodus 15:3–6, 14–16)?

Though the Canaanites in Jericho had a stronger army and a fortified city, they feared for their lives and crouched cowardly inside their walls. They did not fear the Israelites per se. They feared the presence and power of the Israelites' God.

11. How does knowing God is with you affect your life?

12. What does trembling in the face of God indicate in a believer's life?

Rahab knew the peril of protecting the spies. But she also knew that Jericho was ripe for judgment and that by its wickedness it had forfeited all claim to her loyalty. To withstand God and cooperate with an ungodly city would be sheer folly. So she broke with Jericho and aligned herself with Jehovah. It was a risky thing to do, but it was far more dangerous not to align herself with God and His people. She chose Jehovah and rejected Jericho.

13. Describe a time when you took a stand for God in spite of apparent danger.

14. Read Galatians 6:14. What attitude in this verse characterized Rahab?

Wanting some assurance that the Israelites would spare her life when they captured Jericho, Rahab requested "a true token," a symbol that would mark her house as a safe place for her and those who might join her (Joshua 2:12, 13). The spies responded by designating the scarlet cord (rope) by which she lowered them from her house on the wall to the ground for that very purpose (vv. 14–21). Immediately after the spies had left her house, Rahab secured the scarlet rope to her window. It was their promise to her of salvation and life. Rahab then knew the comfort and the courage that came from the presence of the Lord in the midst of desperate circumstances.

How clearly the scarlet rope symbolizes the blood of Christ by which God provides redemption and eternal life! Peter reminded us of the value of the blood: "Forasmuch as ye know that ye were not redeemed with corruptible things, as silver and gold, from your vain conversation received by tradition from your fathers; but with the precious blood of Christ, as of a lamb without blemish and without spot" (1 Peter 1:18, 19). Unless you are saved by the blood of Christ, there is no hope for you. Like the inhabitants of Jericho, you will perish.

15. What would the Canaanites in Jericho have trusted in to help them against the Israelites?

16. What do many nonbelievers in a condemned world depend upon for personal security?

Rahab would be without a city. God would destroy all that she had found comforting in the past. She would need a new home and a new nation with whom to identify.

17. What did God command the Israelites to do with strangers who turned to Jehovah and came into their camps in the Promised Land? Read Numbers 15:14–16.

God knew about Rahab when He gave the commands concerning strangers. Rahab and her family eventually joined the Israelites as the first strangers from Canaan to turn to Jehovah. What a testimony of God's all-encompassing grace!

Rahab begged the spies to save the lives of her family (Joshua 2:13). The spies agreed to do so on the condition that she bring her family "home unto thee" (v. 18).

18. What warning did the spies give to Rahab according to Joshua 2:19 and 20?

Rahab's task would not be easy. Rahab had to persuade her family that safety lay only where the scarlet rope was displayed. They would have to believe that Jehovah would soon destroy Jericho and that He alone could save them. Rahab's responsibility to the members of her family was a life-or-death matter. Would her mission succeed?

19. Read Joshua 6:21–25. How successful was Rahab in persuading members of her family to seek refuge at the end of the scarlet rope?

The presence of God must have made a huge difference in Rahab's life. While the rest of the city fretted, she was at peace. The courage in her heart shone on her face as a quiet confidence. Her family was certainly touched by her testimony of God's grace.

When the two spies returned safely to Joshua and the people of Israel, they told Joshua what they had learned about Jericho and what had happened to them there (Joshua 2:23, 24). Rahab's words to them lay at the heart of their report, because they were such encouraging words. She had reinforced the truth that the Lord had given Israel the land of Canaan (v. 24). They reported what she had told them: "All the inhabitants of the country do faint because of us" (v. 24). Like the two spies, we can anticipate the victories that the Lord has promised. We are on the right side. We have nothing to fear except failure to do His will. His presence gives us courage for the course.

Making It Personal

Like Rahab, we live in a condemned, hopeless world outside God's grace. Our world is a frightening place to live without the courage that God's presence affords.

20. If you are not yet a Christian, you need the eternal safety Jesus offers. He shed His blood to deliver you from your sins and eternal judgment. By trusting in Him as your Savior, you will receive forgiveness and the guarantee of eternal life. Will you trust in Him now?

21. What do your nonbelieving family members and friends read on your face? Do they see the courage that God's presence offers you, or do they see the same hopelessness that *they* have in *their* hearts?

22. What is causing you to fear and lose confidence? Meditate on the following passages, and write a prayer to the Lord about your fears.

Psalm 34

Psalm 46:1

Psalm 91

Proverbs 18:10

Romans 8:15, 16

2 Corinthians 1:3, 4

Philippians 4:6, 7

No Wet Feet

Joshua 3; 4

"Joshua said unto the people, Sanctify your-selves: for to morrow the LORD will do wonders among you" (Joshua 3:5).

Picture yourself aboard a spacecraft on a launching pad. In less than thirty minutes you will blast off and zoom into space, the "final frontier." How do you feel? You are probably extremely nervous. Although this is the adventure you have anticipated for a long time, you don't know what lies ahead. Your confidence in space technology is being tested to the limit. Suddenly only a few seconds remain until liftoff. There's no turning back. You hear, "We have ignition."

The Israelites stood at the Jordan River and peered across at Canaan, their "final frontier." Were they nervous? Were they confident that the Lord would not fail them? There was no turning back. In a matter of moments, the Lord would launch them into Canaan, where unprecedented adventure awaited them.

Getting Started

1. When did you last face a bold new challenge? What, if anything, about that challenge made you nervous?

2. How did confidence in the Lord enable you to meet the challenge? What was the result?

Searching the Scriptures

Canaan, the Promised Land, flowed with milk and honey, but the flowing Jordan River was a formidable barrier to the Israelites' access to the land. Also, after crossing the Jordan, they would encounter strong enemies. However, the Israelites would never reach their objective by relying on their own cleverness or strength, and turning back to the wilderness would result in disaster. Forty years previously, their predecessors had refused to believe that God had given them the Promised Land, and they soon learned that failure to believe Him produces bitter consequences. For the next forty years Israel wandered in the wilderness and witnessed the death of all those over twenty years old.

3. What bitter consequences of unbelief have you read about in the Bible or witnessed in someone's life?

4. Why do you think so many people base their actions on what they think they can do rather than on what God can do through them?

After three days at the Jordan, Israel's officers moved through the ranks of the people issuing a command (Joshua 3:1–3).

5. Read Joshua 3:3. What did the officers command the Israelites to do?

6. Read Exodus 13:21. What had led the Israelites by day in the wilderness?

7. Read Joshua 3:4. Why did the officers instruct the people to stay two thousand cubits (a thousand yards) behind the ark?

Conquering the Canaanites would be a greater *spiritual* exercise than a military one. The Canaanites were pagans. They were devoted to false gods and often sacrificed their children in fire to please their gods. The Devil would empower the Canaanites to fight fiercely against God's people. Joshua wisely prepared the Israelites spiritually for the battles that lay ahead. He commanded them to sanctify (consecrate) themselves, and he assured them that the Lord would perform wonders among them (Joshua 3:5).

8. What do you see as important in preparing to battle "spiritual wickedness in high places": dedication to the Lord or dynamic personality and popular programs? How does Ephesians 6:10–18 help you answer this question?

Joshua commanded the priests to lift the ark and march in front of the people (Joshua 3:6). Then the Lord gave Joshua the last promise and command he would hear outside the Promised Land (vv. 7, 8).

9. What was the promise (Joshua 3:7)?

10. What was the command (Joshua 3:8)?

"And Joshua said unto the children of Israel, Come hither, and hear the words of the LORD your God. And Joshua said, Hereby ye shall know that the living God is among you, and that he will without fail drive out from before you the Canaanites, and the Hittites, and the

Hivites, and the Perizzites, and the Girgashites, and the Amorites, and the Jebusites. Behold, the ark of the covenant of the Lord of all the earth passeth over before you into Jordan" (Joshua 3:9–11).

With these words Joshua promised victory and great blessing. However, the Israelites had to follow the ark of the covenant across the Jordan in submissive obedience. The Lord led the way. They were to follow His lead, trusting Him to direct them in the way of victory.

This was the second time God had brought the Israelites to a formidable water barrier. After the Israelites fled Egypt, He commanded Moses to intentionally lead Israel to camp next to the Red Sea—not a smart military move.

11. Read Exodus 13:21—14:4. Why did God lead the Children of Israel to camp at the Red Sea?

Moses followed the Lord's lead even though the move was on the surface a military blunder (14:3). No matter what logic suggests, we, too, must follow the Lord obediently, submitting to His perfect will. As the Good Shepherd, He always leads us in the right way and provides green pasture (Psalm 23:3; John 10:4, 9).

12. What are some benefits of following the Lord through life?

13. The New Testament instructs believers to follow certain things. Beside each reference below, explain what we ought to follow.

a. Romans 14:19

b. 1 Corinthians 14:1

c. 1 Thessalonians 5:15

d. 1 Timothy 6:11

e. 1 Peter 2:21

Joshua instructed the people to select twelve men, one from each of the twelve tribes, perhaps anticipating what those men would do on the other side of the Jordan (Joshua 3:12). Then he announced a miracle: although the waters of the Jordan were at flood stage, they would part "as soon as the soles of the feet of the priests that bear the ark of the LORD . . . shall rest in the waters of Jordan" (v. 13).

It would take faith for the priests to step into the Jordan, especially at flood stage, but those who follow the Lord must step out in faith. When they do, the Lord performs marvelous deeds. While carrying the ark, the priests waded into the Jordan (vv. 14, 15). The waters parted and "rose up upon an heap" (v. 16). Like the parting of the Red Sea, the Jordan opened like a broad highway, allowing the Israelites to cross near Jericho (vv. 16, 17).

The Lord knew the gravity of the miraculous crossing of the Jordan. After everyone had crossed the river, the twelve men whom Joshua selected from the tribes were to grab a stone from the middle of the Jordan bed (4:1–3).

14. Where were the Children of Israel to put the stones they took from the Jordan (4:3, 20)?

15. How would the sight of the twelve stones from the Jordan affect the forty thousand men in Israel's army each time they left Gilgal for battle? How would it affect the soldiers' wives and children?

16. Whom did God intend reaching with the memorial in Gilgal (4:24)?

17. How did God want the memorial to influence the Israelites' relationship with Him (4:24)?

In essence, the Israelites took a souvenir with them to remember what God had done for them. The tough times in life offer us occasions to pick up some stones as faith builders for future battles. They also offer us opportunities to learn to fear God. As we see Him work, we gain a better understanding of the importance of His commands and the deepness of His love that refuses to let us wander from His side.

God intentionally brings us to a point of facing challenges and obstacles. We can turn and run and experience the devastating consequences, or we can move ahead. Moving ahead requires real faith.

Making It Personal

The Lord calls upon us to follow Him and to step out in faith to do what He commands. Just as crossing the Jordan was a new experience for the Israelites, so the Lord may be directing you into a new experience of faith.

18. What new experience do you believe the Lord may have in store for you?

19. What first step of faith will you take to do what He wants you to do?

20. The Israelites set up a memorial that would help teach their children about the Lord's parting of the Jordan. How can you help your children or grandchildren remember the Lord's marvelous works?

Lesson 4

Getting Ready to Conquer

Joshua 5:1–12

"In whom also ye are circumcised with the circumcision made without hands, in putting off the body of the sins of the flesh by the circumcision of Christ" (Colossians 2:11).

Keri knew she was a Christian, but she also knew she had lived a disobedient life for thirteen years. However, her attitude was beginning to change for the better. She was reading the Bible again, praying daily, and attending church regularly. Tired of her previous lifestyle, she longed for a close relationship with Christ and victory over sin. Having never been baptized, she decided to request baptism. She told her pastor, "I want to be baptized as a public sign of my faith in Christ and intention to obey Him from now on."

Like Keri, the Israelites must have experienced a change of heart when they entered the Promised Land. What they did before conquering Jericho points clearly to their renewed desire to obey the Lord.

Getting Started

1. What indications signify that a believer's life has been renewed?

2. What criteria do you think a believer must meet to enjoy daily victory over sin?

Searching the Scriptures

For almost forty years the Israelites had failed to practice circumcision. During that time the nation had been under judgment; and circumcision, the sign of righteousness, had been omitted. The nation of Israel had ventured into Canaan and was preparing to assault the well-fortified city of Jericho. Only a righteous nation empowered by Jehovah could conquer wicked Jericho. God's first command to His people, therefore, was not to do something to the enemy but to do something to *themselves*.

3. According to Joshua 5:1, what had all the kings of the Canaanites heard?

4. How did they feel after hearing this news?

5. What did the Lord ask Joshua to do in Joshua 5:2?

6. Knowing the Canaanites' attitude, how do you explain that the Israelites delayed the conquest by practicing circumcision?

The practice of circumcision began with Abraham, the father of Israel. When the Lord changed Abram's name to "Abraham" and covenanted to make him "a father of many nations" (Genesis 17:5) and the possessor of the land of Canaan (v. 8), He established circumcision as the sign of the covenant. He commanded circumcision for Abraham and for every male descendant and slave (vv. 10–13). Throughout Israel's history, every baby boy would be circumcised when he was eight days old (v. 12). As the rightful heirs of the Abrahamic Covenant, the Israelites in Canaan accepted circumcision as the sign that set them apart as belonging to the Lord (Joshua 5:7).

Circumcision inflicts pain, and during their recuperation the circumcised Israelites would have been extremely vulnerable if the men of Jericho had attacked them (v. 8). However, the Lord surely protected His people and kept the men of Jericho at home and quaking in their shoes.

God wanted the Israelites to identify with Him outwardly through circumcision. However, His primary concern was that they identify with Him internally. In fact, Moses commanded the Children of Israel to consider their hearts as they were coming to the end of their forty years of wandering in the wilderness.

7. What did Moses command the Israelites to do according to Deuteronomy 10:14–17?

8. Read Colossians 2:11 and 12. What happens to a believer's heart when Christ circumcises it?

9. What ungodly attitudes and desires would be included as part of the "foreskin" of a person's heart?

10. What might have happened to the Israelites if their preparation for battle had not included circumcision of the heart?

In time the Jews perceived circumcision as a guarantee of a right relationship with God. When Paul carried the gospel to the Gentiles and many of them believed on Jesus, he met strong opposition from certain Jews who insisted the Gentile converts be circumcised. However, Paul successfully defended the gospel of grace. He explained that "neither circumcision availeth any thing, nor uncircumcision; but faith which worketh by love" (Galatians 5:6).

11. What religious practices could a believer perform today in an attempt to act like a good Christian?

12. Describe the life of a believer who focuses on looking like a Christian on the outside without regard to his or her heart. How victorious is that person? How much joy and peace does he or she experience?

After the Israelites had recovered physically, the Lord told Joshua that He had rolled away the reproach of Egypt from His people (Joshua 5:9). If the Israelites had never crossed the Jordan, they would have been objects of ridicule in Egyptian conversations, but the Lord had led them into Canaan and retained His honor and Israel's.

13. Name some believers from the Bible who were a reproach, or discredit, to the name of God. How did they affect the unbelievers and believers around them?

Believers who are a reproach to God have forgotten the love God showed to them in delivering them from sin. The Israelites, who had been a reproach to God for forty years, had not observed the Passover since Mount Sinai (Numbers 9:1–5). The passover feast celebrated God's deliverance from the death angel, who passed over their camps in the waning days of their sojourn in Egypt. They renewed this time of reflection and gratitude toward God for deliverance from Egypt as they camped in the plains of Jericho (Joshua 5:10). The Passover helped them to prepare for the coming battles.

14. How would celebrating the passover feast affect the Israelites' spiritual readiness as the city of Jericho literally loomed on the horizon?

God providentially led the Israelites into Canaan at the time of the passover feast. The feast would cause them to reflect on the immeasurable value of the great deliverance the Lord had wrought for them in Egypt. Of course, the greatness of what He had done for them would become increasingly clear as they grew in their relationship to Jehovah.

As New Testament believers, we observe the Lord's Supper in remembrance of the One Who procured our deliverance at Calvary. The more we grow in the Christian life, the more we will appreciate what transpired at Golgotha.

15. How does reflecting on what Christ did on the cross help prepare a believer to face spiritual battles?

After Israel was in Canaan, the land flowing with milk and honey, the Israelites would no longer need manna. The manna ceased, and the people ate their first meal in the new land.

16. What did the Israelites eat when they entered Canaan (Joshua 5:11, 12)?

The variety of food available to the Israelites must have lifted their spirits and given them a taste of the coming blessings of victory. The food was a source of physical strength, too, as the task of conquering the land drew near. God gives us all the spiritual food we need to prepare for spiritual battles. Each Christian must choose whether or not to feed him- or herself with a fresh portion each day.

17. According to Joshua 1:8, what was God's prerequisite for Joshua to enjoy prosperity and success?

18. How would you describe your spiritual diet? Underline the description that applies most accurately.

    a. stale leftovers

    b. an occasional light snack

    c. a starvation amount

    d. a daily feast

Making It Personal

Though God does not require believers to be circumcised to be in fellowship with Him, He still requires circumcision of the heart. Believers are no longer obligated to sin because of the circumcision that Christ performed on their hearts (Colossians 2:11, 12). God wants us to be prepared for battle. If our hearts cling again to that which Christ has cut away, we will be spiritually ineffective.

19. Using the heart diagram on page 37, evaluate the condition of your heart. Ask God to search your heart and reveal to you what you need to let go. In the space between the two hearts, write any fleshly attitudes or desires that you have allowed to control your actions.

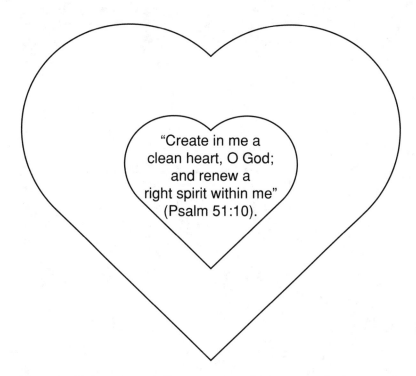

"Create in me a
clean heart, O God;
and renew a
right spirit within me"
(Psalm 51:10).

Trust God's power to deliver you from letting your flesh control your life, and be ready for God to use your renewed heart in tremendous ways.

20. Increasing your diet of spiritual food is absolutely essential in helping you to let go of fleshly desires and attitudes. What can you do to increase your intake of spiritual food this week?

Asking for Directions

Joshua 5:13–15; 6; 7

"And he said, Nay; but as captain of the host of the LORD am I now come. And Joshua fell on his face to the earth, and did worship, and said unto him, What saith my lord unto his servant?" (Joshua 5:14).

Most parents at one point in their lives face the daunting task of putting together a swing set. The one already set up in the store looks so simple to assemble. The one in the box, however, is a different story! All the poles look the same. The nuts and bolts are nearly the same but different enough to keep you scratching your head as you look for a bolt called "B4" to go with a nut called "N9" and a washer called "W2S." The directions for successfully putting together a swing set are complicated, but they are invaluable.

Getting Started

1. When you buy something that requires some assembly, what do you do with the directions?

2. Describe a time when you ignored the directions on how to put a product together. What was the result?

3. What part does safety play in how carefully you follow the directions for a product?

The Israelites were facing something new. They had just crossed the Jordan and were staring down the enemy. Following directions was not only recommended, lives and the success of the whole campaign hinged on it. As their leader, Joshua would fill an important role in seeking and carrying out the Lord's directions.

Searching the Scriptures

Joshua, like many leaders, spent time alone contemplating important decisions. Joshua 5:13 implies that Joshua went close to Jericho, apparently by himself. He had the responsibility to lead God's people into battle. As he stood by Jericho, the immensity of the task became overwhelming. Joshua could see, hear, and perhaps even smell the enemy. God's calling for his life was never more real than at that moment. The spiritual preparations had been made. The people had already eaten from the fruit of the land. Joshua was simply waiting for the Lord's directions.

A stranger silently appeared to Joshua with a drawn sword as if He was ready for hand-to-hand combat. Courageously Joshua approached the stranger and asked Him whose side He was on (v. 13). The stranger identified Himself as the captain of the Lord's host, and Joshua immediately fell on his face before Him.

4. What did Joshua ask the Lord in Joshua 5:14?

Notice that Joshua did not stand up and ask the Lord to bless his plans for storming Jericho. Nor did Joshua ask the Lord for advice or His opinion. Certainly, as the general of the Israelite warriors, Joshua must have had a plan in mind. Whatever it was, he relinquished it to make way for the Lord's instructions.

5. What did Joshua call himself in verse 14?

How easy it would have been for Joshua to call himself the general of the Lord's army, thereby emphasizing the important role he played.

6. Based on how Joshua reacted to the Lord's presence, describe his mind-set.

7. What does Joshua's response to the Lord in the face of a mighty enemy tell you about the importance of involving God in your life as you face spiritual enemies?

The Lord's drawn sword, while at first threatening, became a tremendous source of comfort for Joshua. The Lord and His innumerable host, though unseen, were standing ready for battle with swords drawn. The promise that the Lord had made to Joshua to be with him (Joshua 1:5) became real and concrete.

In 5:15 the Lord preempted His instructions about the battle with an unusual command. He told Joshua to take off his sandals because he was standing on holy ground.

8. What did the Lord communicate to Joshua by calling the land just outside wicked Jericho "holy ground"?

Joshua no longer thought of the land he was standing on as enemy territory. It belonged to the Israelites according to the promise of God. The Canaanites were the real invaders. Joshua and his army were there to take what God had given to them (6:1, 2). They were there to claim the victory! While Joshua stood barefoot, the Lord told him the battle plans (vv. 3–5).

9. Read Joshua 6:2–5. Imagine you were the general instead of Joshua. What would have gone through your mind as you heard the Lord's instructions?

Notice that Joshua did not question the Lord's plan. Neither did he question the Lord's ability. Joshua responded with complete trust. He returned to the people and confidently communicated God's plan. They implemented it immediately and did exactly as God had instructed (vv. 6–15).

Joshua would have never guessed the Lord's plan on his own. He would have never come up with such a scenario for conquering a well-fortified city.

10. Why do you suppose God gave Joshua such an off-the-wall plan?

11. After the marching had ended on the seventh day, Joshua told the people to shout. For what reason did Joshua tell the people to shout (Joshua 6:16)?

There was no way Joshua could take credit for what was about to happen. The plan was obviously the Lord's idea. Taking credit for the imminent victory would have been foolish.

In case the warriors became overzealous in their hunting down and destroying the people of the city, Joshua reminded them to save Rahab and her family (v. 17). He also instructed them to take all the silver, gold, and vessels of brass and iron into the treasury of the Lord (v. 19). Those who kept any valuables for themselves would bring a curse upon the camp of Israel (v. 18).

God was true to His promise. The walls fell flat, and the Israelites entered the city of Jericho to destroy anyone who remained. Rahab was spared, and it seemed as if the Israelites had followed God's commands concerning the valuables. They brought a large haul to the treasury and set fire to the rest of the city (vv. 20–26).

12. Read Joshua 5:14 again and compare it to Joshua 6:27. What did Joshua's actions in 5:14 have to do with what happened to him in 6:27?

The last verse in chapter 6 says that "the LORD was with Joshua." As with Joshua, the Lord is always with us (Matthew 28:20). The question is, are we with the Lord?

13. How can we make sure that we are with the Lord when it comes to living our daily lives?

How elated Joshua must have felt! The Lord, the mighty warrior, was on his side. He could not lose! Or could he?

Chapter 7 opens with astounding news. After watching the Lord hand over the fortified city of Jericho, who would disobey Him and take valuables from the city? Apparently almost no one would dare to do such a thing. Achan was the lone exception. He took some of the spoils for himself and thereby angered the Lord (7:1).

Meanwhile, Joshua proceeded to size up Ai by sending two spies to view the city (v. 2). The report was an encouraging one. The people of Ai were few (v. 3).

14. What advice did the spies give to Joshua (Joshua 7:3)?

Notice that Joshua did not send the spies out to come back with a plan for taking the city, but that is exactly what they did. For whatever reason, Joshua took their advice. The result was disastrous. The small army of Ai chased the Israelites away and managed to kill thirty-six out of the three thousand soldiers that tried to invade the city (vv. 4, 5). While the defeat was a surprise, thirty-six casualties is hardly a heavy loss. More important than the number of deaths was the effect the loss had on the Israelites' hearts.

15. What happened to the Israelites' hearts according to Joshua 7:5?

16. What did Joshua neglect to do between the events of Joshua 6:27 and 7:5? (See 5:14 for a clue.)

The Israelites wondered where the Lord had gone. Was He still by their side? Did He bring them into the land just to set them up for destruction? What would their enemies think? What would happen to the Lord's great name and fame? These questions were going through the minds of Joshua and the elders as they lay with torn clothes before the ark of the Lord (7:6).

Joshua finally spoke his mind and pleaded his case with the Lord. He reminded the Lord how perilous the position of the Israelites had become; the Canaanites would fear them no longer and would move en masse to exterminate them. Joshua seemed to have given up hope. He even wished that they had never entered the land (vv. 7–9)!

God cut Joshua short and told him to get up, cleanse Israel of the sin in the camp, and put the offender to death (vv. 10–15). Joshua did exactly what the Lord commanded him to do (vv. 16–26).

Jericho and Ai presented to Joshua both ends of the battle spectrum. Jericho was on the impossible, there-is-no-way-I-can-handle-this-without-God's-help end of the spectrum. Ai was on the this-should-be-a-breeze end of the spectrum.

17. On what end of the spectrum do most of life's battles fall?

18. If Joshua had an opportunity to speak to you personally about getting ready to fight battles in your life, what do you think he would tell you?

19. God does not talk to us audibly as He did with Joshua, but He does have something to say about our lives and the spiritual battles we face. How does God speak to believers today?

Making It Personal

20. Use the spectrum below to think about the spiritual battles you are currently facing. Write the problems below the spectrum according to how difficult they seem to you.

| A breeze | Impossible! |

21. Think about the problems you listed. From whom have you asked advice or counsel to help you deal with these problems?

22. Describe the conversations you have had with God recently. Are they like the conversations found in Joshua 5:14 or 7:7–9? In other words, are you going to God before acting on your spiritual battles or only after you have failed to win the battle on your own?

Determine to keep your list of spiritual battles current. Take each one of them, those from both sides of the spectrum, to the Lord on a daily basis. Humbly seek His face in all things!

Back to the Basics

Joshua 8:1–35

"Let not mercy and truth forsake thee: bind them about thy neck; write them upon the table of thine heart: so shalt thou find favour and good understanding in the sight of God and man" (Proverbs 3:3, 4).

Football teams at every level of competition—whether high school, college, or professional—work hard at the basic skills required to give them a successful season. It is not uncommon to hear the head coach of a slumping football team explain, "We need to get back to the basics." Similarly, when a Christian experiences a slump in his or her life and encounters defeat, that believer needs to get back to the basics of Christian living.

Getting Started

1. What sports teams have disappointed you because they ignored the basics of the game?

2. What do you consider some basic principles that result in effective Christian living?

Searching the Scriptures

Although Ai was just a little town, it was an enemy town that Israel could not simply ignore. The Israelites must have been discouraged and fearful that the defeat at the hands of the men of Ai foreshadowed additional defeats if they marched farther into Canaan. Sometimes a small setback in our Christian lives can make us fearful of the future. We may begin to despair of serving God. Or we may meet the setback with a careless attitude and tell ourselves to forget it and proceed as planned.

Neither attitude serves us well. If we despair and give up, we will forfeit future blessings. If we dismiss the defeat as inconsequential and proceed without addressing the reason we were defeated, we will fall on our faces again. We ought to pursue the course Israel followed regarding Ai.

The Israelites renewed their obedience to the Lord. He encouraged Joshua to put aside his fear and dismay and to "take all the people of war with thee, and arise, go up to Ai" (Joshua 8:1). He said He had given Ai, its king, his people, and his land to the Israelites (v. 1). Then He outlined His plan for victory (v. 2).

3. What did the Lord command Joshua to do to Ai and its king?

4. What did the Lord command Joshua to do with the spoil and the cattle?

5. The Lord told Joshua to take all the people of war with him. How did this command contrast with Israel's previous effort to take Ai?

Joshua and his men drew the men of Ai into an ambush (vv. 3–15). All the men left Ai in hot pursuit of what they thought was Joshua's entire contingent. At the Lord's command, the designated ambush party ran into Ai and set it ablaze. The men of Ai became trapped between their burning city and the Israelites. They soon fell to Joshua's army, and their king became Joshua's captive (vv. 16–23).

6. Read Joshua 8:24–29. What became of

a. Ai's inhabitants?

b. Ai's cattle and spoil?

c. Ai itself?

d. Ai's king?

7. How many men and women fell to the Israelites?

8. How well had Israel obeyed the Lord in the taking of Ai?

9. What link do you see between obedience and victory in the Christian life?

If the Israelites were to be a victorious people, they could not for a moment forget the foundational truths that God had given them. They had go back to the basics. Joshua was not ignorant of the tremendous challenges confronting his people. There were yet great enemies to face and much land to be possessed, but he was wise enough to pause for a while and give the people opportunity to remember the basis of their fellowship with the Lord. He erected an altar, and the Israelites offered burnt offerings and peace offerings to the Lord (vv. 30, 31). As they meditated on the significance of the offerings, they were reminded of their own unworthiness before the Lord, of God's grace in providing forgiveness, and of the peace between them and God as a result of the sacrifices. Joshua also wrote a copy of the law of Moses on the altar's stones, and he did so "in the presence of the children of Israel" (v. 32). This inscribed law would remind the people that true worship is based on God's Word.

In the light of all this, it certainly is no accident that one of the ordinances given to the church is the ordinance of the Lord's Supper. No matter how spiritually mature a Christian may become, he or she must keep going back in memory to Calvary in the spirit of humility, brokenness, and self-examination and must keep remembering the "Lord's death till he come" (1 Corinthians 11:26).

10. Why is worship meaningless unless it is based on Jesus' sacrifice on the cross?

11. When you meditate on Jesus' sacrifice, what are you most grateful for?

It seems significant that Joshua did not offer the sacrifices upon the altar and then command the people to depart. He had them remain for a full reading of the law of Moses (vv. 33, 34). "There was not a word of all that Moses commanded, which Joshua read not before all the congregation of Israel, with the women, and the little ones, and the strangers that were conversant among them" (v. 35). He wanted his people to know that God expected obedience from them. He wanted even the children to know that the law of Moses included both blessings and cursings and that disobedience would bring chastisement just as surely as obedience would bring blessing.

Most of us know that believers are not "under the law," but we must not forget that the righteousness of the law is to be fulfilled in believers, who walk not after the flesh but after the Spirit (Romans 8:4). We are being altogether Scriptural when we insist that the law of Moses is not binding on a believer in the present age, but we are not being Scriptural when we despise the righteousness of which the law spoke. The Holy Spirit was given to the believer to make him or her capable of righteousness that the law was unable to produce. Obedience to the Lord, therefore, is not a "legalism" of which we must beware but the pathway of holiness that we are able to walk by the power of the Holy Spirit.

12. What do the following verses teach about righteousness?

a. Romans 6:13—We are instructed to yield _____ as "instruments of righteousness unto God."

b. 2 Corinthians 5:21—Our source of righteousness is

c. Ephesians 5:9—The fruit of righteousness may be traced to

d. 2 Timothy 3:16—Our instruction in righteousness comes from

13. What do you consider the greatest threats to righteous living today?

14. Israel was accountable to be holy even in the pagan land of Canaan. How can a believer lead a righteous life in the midst of a morally and spiritually bankrupt culture?

Making It Personal

15. On an ascending scale of 0 to 10, indicate the degree of victory you are experiencing in your Christian life.

16. What fears keep you from obeying the Lord?

17. Write a prayer of commitment, asking God to help you overcome your fears and obey Him.

18. Describe your daily worship of the Lord.

19. List specific ways that you can worship the Lord throughout a typical day.

20. Besides reading and studying God's Word, how else can you revere it?

The High Cost of Compromise

Joshua 9:1–27

"Be ye not unequally yoked together with un-believers: for what fellowship hath righteous-ness with unrighteousness? and what commu-nion hath light with darkness?" (2 Corinthians 6:14).

Dwight L. Moody told the story of a man who had a beautiful canary that sang sweetly. With the coming of spring he felt it a pity to keep the poor bird in the house, so he put it under a tree in front of his house. Before he knew it, a flock of English sparrows gathered under the tree and filled the air with their "chirp, chirp, chirp." The canary quickly picked up the sparrows' chirp. Realizing his mistake, the man took his canary back into the house; but it kept up that "chirp, chirp, chirp." His canary never recovered its sweet notes, he reported.

Believers must be wary of the temptation to compromise. In a world that scorns Christian living, compromise is inevitable for the believer who desires to fit in and downplay or hide his or her distinctiveness as a follower of Christ.

Getting Started

1. How can a Christian befriend the unsaved without becoming like them?

2. What differences should distinguish a Christian from unbelievers?

3. If your unsaved friends were to list five characteristics of your life, what would they list?

Searching the Scriptures

Israel's victories over Jericho and Ai caused great consternation among the kings on the western side of the Jordan River. The Hittites, the Amorites, the Canaanites, the Perizzites, the Hivites, and the Jebusites prepared for war (Joshua 9:1, 2). The inhabitants of the city of Gibeon, however, decided to use cunning instead of armed conflict to ensure their survival (vv. 3–13). They sent to Joshua messengers who pretended they had come from a great distance and sought peace.

4. How did the Gibeonites' ambassadors trick Joshua into believing they had come from a very far country (Joshua 9:3–13)?

5. How suspicious was Joshua of the Gibeonites (Joshua 9:8)?

6. What tragic mistake led to Joshua's acceptance of the Gibeonites' story (Joshua 9:14)?

7. How big a compromise did Joshua think he was making? Consider his decision-making process.

Joshua and Israel's leaders swore to allow the "foreigners," the Gibeonites, to live, thus committing themselves to a direct violation of God's instructions to drive the inhabitants out of the land.

8. What would the Israelites gain from a covenant with the Gibeonites that God had not already offered to them?

9. In what ways are believers tempted to compromise?

10. What do believers try to gain through compromise that they think is better than obedience to the Lord?

Three days after the covenant of peace was made, the Israelites learned that the Gibeonites were their neighbors and "that they dwelt among them" (v. 16). They knew the truth then, but it was too late to do anything about it. In the name of their God they had pledged their word, and they had to live with the bad bargain they had made. They were trapped!

A little carelessness that led to compromise meant that Israel was no longer free to take full possession and enjoyment of the land God had promised to her. She was not totally barred from the blessings of Canaan, but neither was she totally free to enjoy them. Some of her blessings were forfeited, and nothing could ever be done but to mourn the loss. Like Moses, who was denied entrance to Canaan because of one act of disobedience, Israel was going to experience a loss that she could not recoup. The Gibeonites would always be there, occupying part of the land and constituting a threat to the purity of the Israelites' religion.

11. How did the Israelites react when they heard about their leaders' compromise (Joshua 9:18)?

12. What effect can personal compromise have on others?

The Children of Israel had not given their consent to such a betrayal, and they were unhappy with their rulers' lack of spiritual discernment. The Israelites had been called to fight until they had achieved complete victory, but this cheap peace had ruined their cause.

13. In what ways has the church substituted friendship with the world for victory over it?

14. What does a church forfeit by compromising with the world?

15. Pluralism pervades our culture, teaching that all religions, philosophies, and lifestyles are valid and should be accepted and respected. Read Jude 3 and 4 and record the response churches should give to pluralism.

Since the Israelites could not rid themselves of the Gibeonites (Joshua 9:19), they framed a plan for dealing with them. They made the Gibeonites their servants. The Gibeonites would perform the menial tasks of supplying God's people with wood and water (vv. 20, 21). The Gibeonites would furnish wood and water even for "the altar of the LORD" (v. 27). For the moment, the solution to the problem seemed to be a happy one. What was wrong with allowing the people of Gibeon to live with the Israelites and to work with them as long as they, the Israelites, were in absolute control and the pagans were in a subordinate position? They were getting a lot of valuable help from the unbelievers, weren't they?

The answer to those questions is found in God's word to the Israelites at the time of the judges.

16. According to Judges 2:1–4, what trouble did the Gibeonites eventually cause Israel?

Joshua was wrong in thinking that the covenant with the Gibeonites was a small compromise. Eve, Samson, and David are some other Bible characters who made seemingly small compromises that turned out to have grave consequences.

17. What would most believers list as examples of small compromises?

18. What is the danger in thinking that small compromises are manageable and relatively harmless?

19. What does a believer forfeit when he or she fails to obey the Lord fully?

Making It Personal

Compromise is more than just a whimsical decision to disobey God. It is rooted in sinful desires and attitudes. These sinful desires and attitudes must be addressed if a believer is ever to live uncompromisingly.

20. Follow these steps to help you evaluate compromise in your life.

- Draw a tree, including the roots, in the space on page 61.
- On the trunk of the tree, write the word "compromise."

- On the foliage of the tree, record your recent instances of compromise.
- To the left of the foliage, list what you hoped to gain from compromising.
- To the right of the foliage, list the costs of your compromise.

- Determine the sins at the root of your compromises (e.g., fear, pride, lack of trust); write them on the roots of the tree.

Dealing with the root problems on the tree is tantamount to overcoming compromise. Do not be hasty in determining the causes of your compromise. Spend time in prayer, asking God to help you understand what you need to change.

Determine with the Holy Spirit's help to put off the sins that lead to your compromises. Repent of both the compromises and their sinful causes. Use Scripture to determine the attitudes and desires that lead to obedience to the Lord. Trust the Lord to help you live without compromise.

Partners in Battle

Joshua 10:1—11:23

"Joshua said unto them, Fear not, nor be dismayed, be strong and of good courage: for thus shall the LORD do to all your enemies against whom ye fight" (Joshua 10:25).

E veryone has partners. Some partnerships are so vital that the partners depend on each other to survive. Firefighters have a unique bond born of a commitment to help one another in the face of danger. Armed troops are trained to put themselves at risk to save their fellow soldiers. Police officers find comfort in having backup close by. While firefighters, military personnel, and police officers are often trustworthy and make fine partners, no one compares to the partner that Israel had in Jehovah.

Getting Started

1. Imagine you were in a foxhole in the middle of an intense battle. What person would you want with you?

2. What characterizes the person you would choose?

Searching the Scriptures

The Israelites had defeated Jericho and Ai and had made a peace treaty with the inhabitants of Gibeon. When the news of Gibeon's defeat traveled across the land, it caused great worry in the city of Jerusalem. If the Gibeonites, great men of war, had so feared the Israelites that they had refused to fight, there was reason for real alarm. Aware of this dangerous situation, Adonizedec, an Amorite and the king of Jerusalem, sent messengers to enlist the help of the four other kings of the Amorites (Joshua 10:1–4).

3. Read Joshua 10:4 and 5. What was Adonizedec's plan?

Adonizedec put his trust in numbers by pitting five armies against one army. Humanly speaking, Adonizedec's plan made sense. From his perspective he had a partnership guaranteed to win because of sheer strength.

4. What forces of evil sometimes team up against believers?

5. How have Satan and his allies threatened you?

The five kings had a stranglehold on Gibeon, so the Gibeonites sent an SOS to Joshua (Joshua 10:6). How would Joshua respond? Would he honor his agreement with the Gibeonites, or would he let them perish at the hands of the Amorites?

Quickly Joshua led his men of war from Gilgal to join the battle against Adonizedec at Gibeon (v. 7). He was facing one of the most crucial battles of his military career, and he knew it. The Lord told

Joshua to "fear them not" (v. 8). Obviously, five armies at once was a big step up from Ai and even from Jericho. Fear threatened to dominate Joshua's mind.

6. What reason did the Lord give to Joshua for not fearing (v. 8)?

Notice that the Lord did not tell Joshua to "fear them not" because He would take care of the armies by Himself. God implied in His words that He expected Joshua and his army to engage in battle as an ingredient to victory.

7. What does Ephesians 6:10–13 say about the partnership it takes to win spiritual battles?

8. Read Romans 8:37 and 1 John 4:4. How would you describe the victory God has promised believers?

Joshua launched a surprise attack on the five kings (Joshua 10:9). Perhaps the light of day had not begun to dawn when Joshua's forces struck the enemy. The Lord cast the Amorites into confusion, and Israel killed many enemy soldiers. The rest fled westward through a narrow pass leading to Bethhoron. Israel pursued the panicked enemy to the southwest and struck them down near Azekah and Makkedah (v. 10).

9. What did the Lord do to facilitate victory, according to Joshua 10:11?

What an encouragement to the army of Israel! The men could actually see physical evidence that the Lord was indeed fighting with them. As the day of battle drew long, Joshua needed extended daylight to wipe out the Amorites. Though God had killed many of the enemy soldiers with the hailstones, much of the enemy remained.

10. Why did God not kill all of the enemy soldiers with the hailstones?

Since there were many soldiers yet to defeat, Joshua petitioned the Lord for a miracle and commanded the sun and moon to stand still (v. 12). What boldness!

11. What gave Joshua the right to command the sun and moon to stand still?

12. What did Christ promise to believers in John 14:13 and 14?

13. What must be true of a believer's life and request before he or she can claim this promise?

The Lord granted Joshua's request. The sun stood still overhead for about a day, the time Israel needed to battle the Amorites (Joshua 10:13). This day would go down in history as an unprecedented, never-to-be repeated phenomenon (v. 14).

14. Joshua's army and the Lord partnered together to defeat the Amorites. How can Christians partner with the Lord to accomplish great things?

Explanations have been offered for the day the sun stood still. Suggestions range from an eclipse, to a thick cloudbank blocking the sun, to refraction of the sun's rays. However, none of these suggestions accounts for the extended time Joshua received for finishing off the enemy. It seems the Lord slowed the earth's rotation. Instead of making a full rotation in twenty-four hours, the earth rotated once in forty-eight hours.

15. What disastrous effects of changing the earth's rotation did the Lord prevent during that long day?

Somehow the five Amorite kings were able to flee to a cave. However, they could run and hide only for a brief time. Joshua learned where they were hiding, and he quickly took action (vv. 15–27). Joshua dramatized the execution of the five cowardly kings: he had each of the captains of his army stand with a foot on the neck of one of the kings. With this dramatic show, Joshua bolstered the army's courage once again.

16. Read Joshua 10:25. Which enemies did Joshua say the Lord would defeat?

God would continue to help the Israelites as long as they continued to fight. For a while, they did exactly that. Joshua's military success over the Amorites sealed the fate of southern Canaan. With lightning speed Israel attacked enemy cities and destroyed their military capability (vv. 28–42).

17. Read Joshua 10:42. Why was Joshua able to defeat the enemy and claim southern Canaan?

After mopping up southern Canaan, Joshua and his fighting men returned to Gilgal, their base camp, where they had reinstated circumcision and observed the Passover (v. 43; also see Joshua 5).

18. Why is it especially important to return to the place of worship after experiencing a spiritual victory?

News of Israel's victories in the south aroused the northern kings to action (Joshua 11:1–5). They marshaled their forces in vast numbers to fight Israel. Seeing such a vast enemy equipped with horses and chariots must have frightened Joshua, but the Lord encouraged him, saying, "Be not afraid because of them: for to morrow about this time will I deliver them up all slain before Israel" (v. 6).

Encouraged, Joshua took the fight to the enemy, engaging them near Merom. He chased the enemy eastward and westward, eventually turning northward and southward; and obeying the Lord's instructions, he hamstrung the enemy's horses and burned their chariots (vv. 7–9).

19. Why would God ask the Israelites to kill horses and burn chariots when they offered them an advantage militarily? (See Psalm 20:7.)

Sweeping through the north, Joshua and his soldiers destroyed Hazor, Canaan's largest city, and burned it to the ground (Joshua 11:10, 11). They defeated city after city and conquered Canaan so decisively that verse 15 states, "As the LORD commanded Moses his servant, so did Moses command Joshua, and so did Joshua; he left nothing undone of all that the LORD commanded Moses."

Joshua 11:16–23 reports that the Lord had brought the Canaanites en masse against Israel so Israel would defeat them. Truly what may seem to be adversities teaming up against us is actually the Lord's orchestration of events to bring Him glory and to exercise our faith.

Making It Personal

20. What spiritual battles are you facing right now?

21. How victorious have you been in your spiritual battles?

22. Look at the following chart and mark the statements that best describe your life.

Defeated?		Victorious?
I no longer try to win my spiritual battles.	OR	I am proactive in fighting my spiritual battles.
I am often discouraged and hopeless when facing spiritual battles.	OR	I face spiritual battles with courage and hope.
I deal with spiritual losses by just asking God to forgive me.	OR	I deal with spiritual losses by confessing and forsaking my sin.
I do not use God's Word while facing spiritual battles.	OR	I memorize and meditate on God's Word daily as my spiritual battle preparation.
I feel helpless in the midst of spiritual battles.	OR	I rely on the Holy Spirit in the midst of battles.
I dread talking to God because I am so defeated spiritually.	OR	I talk to God about the battles I am facing, asking Him for strength for victory.
I doubt that I will ever be spiritually strong enough to be victorious.	OR	I have a deep faith in God's ability to grant me victory.

Notice that the defeated person is going it alone, with no partner. The victorious Christian is active in the battle but reliant upon and trusting in the Lord.

23. How can you engage in battle and rely on your Partner, the Lord, more fully?

Life Begins at Eighty-five

Joshua 13:1—14:15

"Hebron therefore became the inheritance of Caleb the son of Jephunneh the Kenezite unto this day, because that he wholly followed the LORD God of Israel" (Joshua 14:14).

When a news reporter asked a one-hundred-year-old man the secret of longevity, the old fellow replied, "Keep on breathing."

Breathing is definitely essential to living, but living with a sense of purpose makes breathing worthwhile. In spite of a growing tendency to underutilize the skills and knowledge of older citizens, people in their sixties, seventies, and beyond have much to offer society. And God expects senior saints to keep serving Him. There is no such thing as retirement from the Lord's work. His work gives us a never-ending purpose for living. This lesson features two energetic men who had served the Lord vigorously in their youth and were still doing so in their twilight years.

Getting Started

1. Name some items that become more and more useless with age.

2. What is the common belief about the usefulness of believers as they age?

Searching the Scriptures

Joshua had become old, perhaps one hundred years old by this point (Joshua 13:1). The Lord reminded him of this fact, and He stated that much land in Canaan remained to be possessed.

3. Read through the list of territories yet to be possessed (Joshua 13:2–6). What would you suggest to Joshua as the best way to deal with the problem of unclaimed land?

Following God's command, Joshua allocated parcels of territory to the tribes of Israel (13:7—14:5). In essence, Joshua was changing his position from general of the Israelite army to mentor and motivator for each of the tribes.

4. How much older was Joshua than the oldest Israelites (Numbers 14:29–33)?

Israel had defeated many formidable enemies, but many battles lay ahead. However, each tribe had to battle the foes in the portion of Canaan assigned to it and to conquer its own land. No tribe would necessarily have the help of any other tribe; each would have to conquer its own enemies and trust God to give it its territory. In some respects, that might prove more difficult than the great military campaigns in which all the tribes had participated together. Each tribe would recognize the smallness of its number, and each Israelite male would sense more strongly his own responsibility in the success of the venture. A few fainthearted men of little faith would be more capable of causing some of the tribes to fail than had ever been true before. Each tribe needed all its men to be strong and push forward in spite of the fierceness of the battle or the strength of the enemy.

Joshua knew that he would not lead Israel to conquer all of the land. The leaders of the tribes and the captains of his army would have to finish the job.

5. While conquering the land, what did Joshua do to encourage the captains of his army to take up the mantle of leadership (Joshua 10:22–27)?

Besides God, no one was of more value to the Israelites at that point in their history than Joshua. He was well acquainted with both chastening and blessing from the hand of God. He had a breadth of experience that no one else could match.

6. Think back over the life of Joshua. What had he witnessed and accomplished up to that point in his life?

7. What harm could have come from Joshua's continuing to lead the army of Israel without pressing the tribes into leadership before his death?

8. What happens when older, seasoned church members continue to serve but do not help to mentor and encourage younger members?

Joshua knew that trying to continue in his role as general would ultimately not help the Israelites. He had to pass the baton to the younger generation.

9. Paul took time to prepare younger men for the ministry. How did Paul describe his mentoring relationship with Timothy in Philippians 2:19–22?

10. How did Timothy respond to Paul's mentoring according to 2 Timothy 3:10 and 11?

11. What can the church do to encourage mentoring relationships between older and younger members?

Caleb was another older person who demonstrated the value of those with a lifelong history of faithfulness to God. Caleb had searched Canaan forty-five years earlier as a spy with Joshua and had stood with him to urge the Israelites to invade Canaan with confidence in the Lord. Once in the Promised Land, he boldly requested Mount Hebron from Joshua (Joshua 14:12, 13). During the long, trying years in the wilderness, Caleb had cherished a promise from God (v. 6). Caleb implored Joshua, "Now therefore give me this mountain, whereof the LORD spake in that day; for thou heardest in that day how the Anakims were there, and that the cities were great and fenced: if so be the LORD will be with me, then I shall be able to drive them out, as the LORD said" (v. 12).

12. Read Numbers 13:22, 28, and 31–33. Of the inhabitants of the Promised Land, whom did the spies fear the most?

Caleb, the second oldest man in all of Israel, asked Joshua for the opportunity to take on the biggest and the "baddest" people in all of Canaan.

13. What had God done for Caleb physically during the previous forty-five years (Joshua 14:11)?

God prepared Caleb for the rigorous task of taking down the giants of Hebron. However, it was not his physical strength that made the difference. Surely younger men could best Caleb in a wrestling match. The difference for Caleb was his deep devotion to God and spiritual strength. He had kept his eyes on the goal and had followed the Lord, even when the hearts of the rest of his countrymen melted (vv. 7–9). Caleb had allowed nothing to discourage him in spite of the factors that had threatened his faith. Believing deeply in God's faithfulness, he succeeded where others failed, and he "wholly followed the LORD God of Israel" (v. 14). Caleb was a man who stuck like glue to the promises of God.

The long delay in entering Canaan might have tossed many a man into the pit of despair, but Caleb was willing to bide God's time. The dissension he saw among God's people might have filled him with disgust and caused him to throw up his hands at the seeming hopelessness of the situation; but if God had not given up on His people, neither would Caleb. He knew giants lived in well-fortified cities in the territory he requested. But he also knew the Lord was stronger than the enemies and would enable him to rout them (v. 14). His confidence in the Lord was as firm at eighty-five as it had been at forty. And old age had not diminished his eagerness to defeat the enemy.

14. What did Caleb's boldness and deep trust in the Lord in the face of a powerful enemy do for Othniel, Caleb's nephew? (See Joshua 15:13–17 and Judges 3:7–11).

15. What opportunities do older believers forfeit by refusing to get involved in the most prevalent challenges facing the church?

16. What attitude should younger generations in the church have toward those of the older, more mature generations?

17. a. Read 1 Corinthians 15:58. What age restrictions, if any, do you find in this verse?

   b. What does this verse imply about the value of the service of believers, including older generations?

We read that Joshua blessed Caleb and gave him Hebron for an inheritance (Joshua 14:13). "Hebron therefore became the inheritance of Caleb the son of Jephunneh the Kenezite unto this day, because that he wholly followed the LORD God of Israel" (v. 14).

Making It Personal

As older saints, Joshua and Caleb filled important roles in the establishment of the Promised Land.

18. a. If you are a seasoned believer, what could you contribute to the ministry of your church in the area of mentoring?

   b. Choose someone younger than you who needs a spiritual mentor. Offer your ministry to that person. Write the person's name below.

19. a. If you are an older saint, what best describes your part in the ministry of the church? Choose one of the following descriptions:

__ Disinterested
__ Cheering from the stands
__ A casual participant
__ Playing a vital role

   b. What, if anything, do you need to do to become more active in service for the Lord?

20. a. If you are a younger person, what adjustments, if any, do you need to make in your attitude toward the value of older believers in the church?

   b. Who would be a good mentor for you?

   Plan to ask that person to meet with you about developing a mentoring relationship.

Forward, March!

Joshua 15:1—17:18

"Fight the good fight of faith, lay hold on eternal life, whereunto thou art also called, and hast professed a good profession before many witnesses" (1 Timothy 6:12).

Sports fans know that winning one Super Bowl or Stanley Cup does not guarantee an unbroken string of victories the next year. In a single season fans have seen Super Bowl champions fall as flat as a deflated football and Stanley Cup champions turn as cold as the ice under their skates. As in every ongoing endeavor, sports teams cannot afford to coast or become overconfident. Similarly, Christian living involves diligence and confidence in the Lord, because a single victory does not guarantee a string of victories.

Getting Started

1. What team, company, or ministry have you known to tumble from success to failure?

2. What contributed to this fall?

3. What Bible characters tumbled from spiritual heights to distressingly low points?

4. What contributed to their fall?

Searching the Scriptures

The Israelites had invaded Canaan and had been blessed by God in almost all they had tried to do. They had achieved victory over powerful enemies that had tried to halt their forward rush across the land. They had been eminently successful up to the point of the mopping-up operations that were assigned to the various tribes. Then they began to fail. Having won the greater battles, they lost the lesser ones.

5. Read the following verses. Record what Joshua wrote about the incompleteness of the conquest of the land.

   a. Joshua 15:63

   b. Joshua 16:10

   c. Joshua 17:12

The Israelites quit trying to achieve total victory and settled down to coexist with their enemies. Their satisfaction with partial victory led to complacency and eventually to sin.

6. According to Judges 3:5–7, what trouble did the Canaanites eventually cause the Israelites?

Our past victories do not by any means guarantee future successes. We may have tasted the delights of spiritual conquest time and again. We may have leaped over every high hurdle the enemy placed in the road. We may have crushed every opponent who dared to interpose himself between us and our God-appointed goals. We may have moved successively from one triumph to another; and then, quite unexpectedly, we may have failed. There are no assurances that defeat is out of range for those conquerors who have moved previously in the sphere of victory. God's power is always available to God's people, but there is no guarantee that they will avail themselves of it.

Though Israel was supposed to completely drive out the Canaanites from the land, God in His sovereignty kept Israel from driving all of them out (Judges 3:1). The presence of the Canaanites gave the Israelites an opportunity to prove their loyalty to the Lord (v. 4).

7. How is living the Christian life like the Israelites' lives in the partially claimed land?

8. What dangers lurk for the Christian who becomes complacent with past victories and tries to coast through life?

Caleb stood in stark contrast to the complacent one who failed to drive out the inhabitants of the land. Caleb boldly took his inheritance even though it was inundated with the Anakim, people famous for their size and strength.

A husband and the land he fought to obtain were not the only inheritance Achsah received from her father. Achsah also gained a spiritual heritage from him.

9. What evidence of Achsah's bold faith do you see in Joshua 15:18 and 19?

10. What counsel would you give to parents who have chosen spiritual complacency in order to concentrate their energies on giving a generous material inheritance to their children?

While Achsah asked Caleb for additional land after her husband, Othniel, had driven out the inhabitants of Debir, the tribe of Ephraim and half the tribe of Manasseh asked Joshua for more land too. They were not happy that Joshua had given them only one portion of land on the western side of the Jordan. (The other half-tribe of Manasseh had requested land on the eastern side of the Jordan River and had received it.)

11. Read Joshua 17:14. On what basis did the people of Ephraim and Manasseh think they deserved more land?

Joshua pointed out to Ephraim and Manasseh that if indeed they were so great, they should have no trouble creating enough room in the land that God had given them.

12. Read Joshua 17:15. What solution did Joshua give to Ephraim and Manasseh?

The people who complained about the small size of their inherited land were not even occupying the land they had received. They could expand into the hill country if only they would cut down the trees. Also, plenty of land in the valley of Jezreel could be theirs if only they would drive out the Canaanites who still possessed it (v. 16).

If they didn't have enough room, it was their own fault. With God as their helper they could cut down the trees in the hills and drive out the strong enemy in the valley. The task was not beyond their ability to perform, and they were expected to perform it. In no other way could they move into the fullness and abundance that God had provided for them.

Those who become spiritually complacent often become complainers about the lack of spiritual inheritance they have. As they look at others who have continued to march forward in their spiritual lives, they have a "why do they get all the privileges" type of attitude.

13. Read Matthew 25:14–23. On what basis does the Lord grant additional privileges?

14. What spiritual privileges belong to those who continue to march forward in their spiritual lives?

Joshua was much too wise to coddle the Israelites, who had asked for an easy way out of their difficulty. Instead of that, he insisted that they live up to what they claimed to be and were able to be. They had said that they were a great people and that God had greatly blessed them. Refusing to take issue with that, he said, "Thou art a great people, and hast great power: thou shalt not have one lot only: but the mountain shall be thine; for it is a wood, and thou shalt cut it down: and the outgoings of it shall be thine: for thou shalt drive out the Canaanites, though they have iron chariots, and though they be strong" (Joshua 17:17, 18). The house of Joseph's "lot" could have been doubled if Joseph's children had exercised their muscles and exhibited some courage. It was as simple as that!

When a pastoral candidate asked the pulpit committee if the members of the congregation were committed to working diligently for the Lord, the chairman replied, "Our church is *full* of willing workers. Some are willing to work, and the rest are willing to let them." Those who are spiritually complacent and complaining about their spiritual privileges hurt the forward motion of a church.

Obviously, nothing worthwhile gets accomplished in personal lives or in a church without hard work, but the Lord works with us to reach the goals that His will defines.

15. What did Paul command the Philippians in Philippians 2:12?

16. According to Philippians 2:13, what makes obeying the command in Philippians 2:12 worthwhile?

Making It Personal

Complacency is a real danger for those who have experienced spiritual victory. "Forward, march!" is the clarion call for all believers. Those who decide to coast or rest on their laurels after victory will soon find themselves defeated.

17. What has happened in your life since your last spiritual victory? How complacent have you become?

18. a. Name a person you think is strong spiritually.

b. What is your attitude toward that person? Do you look at him or her as an example to live up to? Or do you complain about not being as spiritually strong as he or she is?

19. What do you need to do today to either begin or continue to march forward in your spiritual life? Write out your steps of action.

(1)

(2)

(3)

(4)

(5)

A Controversial Altar

Joshua 22:1–34

"Behold, how good and how pleasant it is for brethren to dwell together in unity" (Psalm 133:1).

A young believer and a mature believer were enjoying the warmth of a campfire after a long day of fishing. The young man confided in his older friend that he was seriously thinking about skipping Sunday services. "I could use the time invested in church services to get some things done around the house. I could tune in to a televised church service and turn up the volume so I wouldn't miss a thing," he explained.

The mature believer pushed a small burning log out of the roaring fire, resting it on the ground several feet from the fire. "Let's see how long this log can keep glowing apart from the rest of the logs," he suggested.

Within minutes the young man understood the value of staying united with fellow believers.

Getting Started

1. What benefits do you derive from worshiping and serving the Lord alongside other believers?

2. Have you known believers who dropped out of church and just stayed home or engaged in work or pleasure instead of corporate worship? What became of them?

3. What kinds of things might threaten the unity of a body of believers?

4. What kinds of things help to build unity in a local church?

Searching the Scriptures

Seeing good pastures in the land of Jazer and Gilead, the tribes of Reuben and Gad in Moses' day had requested of him, "Let this land be given unto thy servants for a possession, and bring us not over Jordan" (Numbers 32:5).

Moses had replied, "Shall your brethren go to war, and shall ye sit here? And wherefore discourage ye the heart of the children of Israel from going over into the land which the LORD hath given them?" (vv. 6, 7).

The two tribes, however, insisted that they preferred the eastern side of the Jordan River. If only Moses would grant them permission to do so, they said, they would cross the Jordan with the other tribes and fight alongside them until the land of Canaan was securely in Israel's hands.

Moses agreed, "If ye will do this thing, if ye will go armed before the LORD to war, and will go all of you armed over Jordan before the LORD, until he hath driven out his enemies from before him, and the land be subdued before the LORD: then afterward ye shall return, and be guiltless before the LORD, and before Israel; and this land shall be your possession before the LORD" (vv. 20–22).

Joshua was aware of the promise Moses had made to Reuben, Gad, and the half-tribe of Manasseh, so he called those tribes to him and said, "Ye have kept all that Moses the servant of the LORD commanded you, and have obeyed my voice in all that I commanded you: ye have not left your brethren these many days unto this day, but have kept the charge of the commandment of the LORD your God. And now the LORD your God hath given rest unto your brethren, as he promised them: therefore now return ye, and get you unto your tents, and unto the land of your possession, which Moses the servant of the LORD gave you on the other side Jordan" (Joshua 22:2–4).

5. Read Joshua 22:5 and 6. What did Joshua exhort the departing tribes to do?

6. Why is it important for church members to know what is expected of them both inside and outside the church?

Arriving at the crossing of the Jordan, the two and one-half tribes hesitated before continuing the journey home. After they crossed the river, they would be cut off from the fellowship with their brethren that they had previously enjoyed. That river was a natural barrier, and it could be that eventually the two and one-half tribes would not be recognized as belonging to the rest of Israel. What could they do to symbolize their oneness with the tribes that were occupying Canaan proper? What could they establish as a continuing witness that they belonged to the nation of Israel and the people of God?

7. Read Joshua 22:10. What did the two and one-half tribes construct to symbolize their unity with the other tribes?

8. How does Joshua 22:10 describe the structure?

It did not take long for word about the impressive altar to reach the other tribes. When they heard about the altar, they immediately concluded that the two and one-half tribes were expecting to offer sacrifices on the altar and had rebelled against the Lord. To set up another place of worship was evidence of apostasy, and "the whole congregation of the children of Israel gathered themselves together at Shiloh, to go up to war against them" (v. 12). They had very little confidence in their brethren, it seems, and they were quick to believe the worst about them. They girded on their swords even before they knew if they had cause for battle. They had zeal to spare but very little knowledge to go with it. On the basis of scanty information, they had come to a definite conclusion that amounted to a false judgment about their own kinsmen.

9. What precautions should a congregation take when deciding if a member should receive church discipline (Matthew 18:15–17)?

10. What are some unjustifiable reasons to leave a church?

11. Is there a justifiable reason to leave a church? If so, what is it?

As the Israelites mobilized for war, someone must have interjected a word of caution and advised sending a committee to investigate their brethren's reasons for building the controversial altar. Perhaps Joshua himself suggested this wise course of action. The committee was composed of Phinehas, the son of Eleazar the priest, and ten princes (or rulers) from the nine and one-half tribes who had their inheritances on the western side of the Jordan River (Joshua 22:13, 14). This surely was in

keeping with God's command in Deuteronomy 13 to carefully investigate those who were suspected of heresy. Those suspected of trying to
lead God's people away from Him were to receive every fair chance of
clearing themselves, but they were not to be tolerated after it was firmly
established that they were guilty. The penalty for apostasy was death.

12. How should a congregation respond to apostasy and heresy
(2 Thessalonians 3:14, 15; 2 Timothy 3:13, 14; Titus 3:10)?

The committee investigated the situation the two and one-half tribes
had created (Joshua 22:15–20).

13. How would you describe the committee's attitude when it con-
fronted the two and one-half tribes?

14. Read Galatians 6:1. What attitude should believers have when
they seek to restore a fallen brother or sister?

15. Read Joshua 22:20. What had recently happened to Israel that
caused the people to be so concerned about fidelity to the one true
God? What were the consequences?

16. Why would minding their own business have meant danger to
the nine and one-half tribes?

17. What is dangerous about letting sin fester in a church under the guise of "I'm minding my own business"? (See 1 Corinthians 5.)

When the committee from the nine and one-half tribes discovered that Reuben and Gad had not departed from Jehovah, they were pleased and relieved. Speaking for the whole committee, Phinehas said, "This day we perceive that the LORD is among us, because ye have not committed this trespass against the LORD: now ye have delivered the children of Israel out of the hand of the LORD" (Joshua 22:31). In due time the committee reported the good news back to the other Israelites, and war was averted (vv. 32, 33). The two and one-half tribes crossed the Jordan, leaving behind them the altar of testimony as a standing monument of their faith in Jehovah as God and of their oneness with all the other tribes of the Children of Israel.

Christ established a church on earth so believers would get together, stay together, and work together. It is serious, therefore, to forsake "the assembling of ourselves together" (Hebrews 10:25). We must remind ourselves that we are not simply a fellowship of persons with a common interest, such as the Audubon Society or a law fraternity or a garden club, though we may appear to be such to an outsider. We are a company of God's children, who have been made partakers of the divine nature and are experiencing a shared life. Our assemblies, therefore, are gatherings of redeemed people through whom Christ's life and love flow. We are members of Christ's Body (1 Corinthians 12:12). Our spiritual gifts vary, but we are one body. We must not "go it alone." We must be so identified with the fellowship of believers that no one who knows us will ever have occasion to doubt it.

18. According to John 13:35, how will the world know that believers are Jesus' disciples?

19. How well do you think your congregation measures up to the test of discipleship given in John 13:35? If you believe there is room for improvement, how might the congregation improve its score?

Making It Personal

20. Memorize Psalm 133:1 this week. What can you do to contribute to your church's unity?

21. Do you believe a certain person is disrupting the unity of your church? If so, commit to pray for that person; then meet with him or her and listen carefully to what that person says before making a judgment.

22. What do you most appreciate about God's family of believers?

23. How will you respond the next time someone begins to gossip about a fellow believer?

An Old Soldier Speaks from the Heart

Joshua 23:1–16

"Take good heed therefore unto yourselves, that ye love the LORD your God" (Joshua 23:11).

On April 11, 1951, President Truman relieved General MacArthur of his command in South Korea. The revered general arrived home to a hero's welcome and received an invitation to address the Congress. At the close of his speech to Congress, General MacArthur stated, "Old soldiers never die; they just fade away."

Thousands of years before General MacArthur uttered those famous words, General Joshua gathered all the tribes of Israel together at Shechem. It was a solemn assembly that included Israel's elders, leaders, judges, and officials, all of whom would hear Joshua's closing remarks to the nation. Soon afterward Joshua died, but he did not fade away. His life and words recorded in the Bible have challenged and strengthened the faith of God's people throughout subsequent history.

Getting Started

1. Describe a memorable speech or sermon you've heard.

2. What made it so memorable?

3. If you knew you had only a few minutes to live, what two things would you like to tell your loved ones?

    (1)

    (2)

Searching the Scriptures

Many years had slipped by since Joshua had led the Children of Israel in the fight for Canaan. For a long time God's people had been occupying the Land of Promise, and Joshua had continued to give them the benefit of his wise counsel and leadership. The time came when he realized his life would soon end. "I am old and stricken in age," he said (Joshua 23:2). He felt constrained to charge his people to be faithful to the Lord after his departure. He had been an outstanding and noble example of consistency and faithfulness, and his words were powerful because the weight of his own godly life was behind them.

Joshua's speech informed the Israelites that they would dispossess the remaining Canaanites only if they carefully obeyed the law of Moses and were faithful to the Lord (vv. 3–8).

4. Read Joshua 23:3 and 4. How does reflecting on the Lord's goodness in the past encourage you to serve Him faithfully today?

5. What positive counsel did Joshua give (v. 6)?

6. When had he received this same counsel?

7. What commands did Joshua issue in Joshua 23:7?

8. What does it mean to "cleave unto the LORD" (Joshua 23:8)?

If courage is the virtue that is required for obedience to the Lord, love is the motivating force that supplies it. "Take good heed therefore unto yourselves, that ye love the LORD your God," said Joshua (v. 11). What would be the use of telling people to obey a God they did not love? What reason would there be for enduring the abuse and opposition of the pagans in the land if they had no genuine desire to please the Lord, Whom they were supposed to affectionately adore?

On a cold, bitter, wintry night in New York City, a commuter train conductor was receiving tickets at the gate. In the line of duty he had to stop the rushing passengers and demand their tickets. This meant their taking off warm gloves and exposing their hands to the cold, biting wind, a process calculated to sharpen tempers and tongues. Several uncomplimentary remarks were hurled at the conductor. A friend, seeing his plight, remarked, "You're not very popular tonight, are you?" The conductor smiled, pointed to the lighted windows of the railroad's general offices, and replied, "I only want to be popular up there."

That is precisely the attitude of a believer who wants to please the Lord he or she loves. Neither the world's approval nor its abuse means much to that believer; he or she desires only to "cleave unto the LORD" with all of his or her heart. This is what love requires.

9. According to Joshua 23:10, what would happen if the Israelites held fast to the Lord because they loved Him?

10. How has loving the Lord and obeying His Word kept you from spiritual disaster?

Joshua warned that coexisting with the enemy would lead to compromise. Before long the Israelites would intermarry with the Canaanites (v. 12), and those unions would plague Israel. The Canaanites would remain in the land and become "snares and traps," "scourges" in the Israelites' sides, and "thorns" in their eyes (v. 13). Ultimately the Israelites would perish from the land.

11. Are Christians supposed to be a part *of* the culture or *apart from* the culture? Explain.

12. Do you think churches are becoming "Canaanized"? Defend your answer.

13. What future do you predict for a "Canaanized" church?

Joshua testified that he would soon die, but he affirmed the truth that God had faithfully kept His word to the Israelites. "Not one thing hath failed of all the good things" He had spoken concerning His people (v. 14). The Israelites could depend upon the Lord to keep His promises. And so can we.

Paul assured Titus, a young pastor, that God cannot lie (Titus 1:2). This assurance would fortify Titus for ministry to a people notorious for lying. It would encourage him to know that those who believed on Jesus would receive eternal life and forgiveness, just as God had promised. It would encourage him to know that God would never fail him.

14. What promises are you relying on today because God always keeps His Word?

The fact that God keeps His Word is a double-edged sword. He will stand by His promises to bless those who are faithful to Him, and He will also stand by His promises to discipline those who are unfaithful to Him. Joshua told Israel, "It shall come to pass, that as all good things are come upon you, which the LORD your God promised you; so shall the LORD bring upon you all evil things [calamities], until he have destroyed you from off this good land which the LORD your God hath given you" (Joshua 23:15).

The New Testament echoes this warning. If a Christian sows wild oats, the Lord will start up His threshing machine. His purpose is to perform remedial discipline so His wayward child will return to close fellowship with Him. The writer of Hebrews referred to this disciplinary action.

Read Hebrews 12:5–11.

15. What emotion does God exhibit in discipline?

16. What does our receiving divine discipline prove?

17. Why does God discipline His children?

18. What actions should we take when we are disciplined?

General Joshua warned Israel that transgressing God's covenant by serving and bowing down to false gods would incite His wrath and cause Him to remove the people of Israel from the Promised Land (Joshua 23:16).

19. What eventually happened to Israel because of idolatry?

20. Why do believers today need the apostle John's admonition in 1 John 5:21, "Little children, keep yourselves from idols"?

Making It Personal

21. Joshua passed along to the Israelites wisdom he had acquired during a long lifetime of honoring God. What main lessons about God and Christian living have you learned since becoming a Christian?

22. What harmful associations or false gods, if any, do you need to eliminate from your life?

23. How thankful are you for God's faithfulness? How will you show your gratitude?

Lesson 13

A Clear Choice

Joshua 24:1–33

"If it seem evil unto you to serve the LORD, choose you this day whom ye will serve; . . . but as for me and my house, we will serve the LORD" (Joshua 24:15).

C hoices bombard us every day. It is impossible to live through a day without making choices. Shall we wear blue or khaki? What shall we order from the lunch menu—a cheeseburger or a lean turkey sandwich or a salad? Shall we buy a Ford or a Chevy or neither? Shall we purchase gas now or drive a few more miles before purchasing it? Choices like these carry only minor consequences.

However, some other choices are weighty and carry major consequences. If we choose to marry an unbeliever, we may live with a lifetime of regret and hardship. If we choose to walk off the job, we may not be able to meet our housing and medical expenses. If we choose to dishonor the Lord, we will experience guilt and restlessness. However, if we choose to honor Him, life will overflow with His joy and peace.

Choices are important! They must be made. We cannot escape the reality of choices.

Getting Started

1. What difficult choices have you had to make recently? What resulted from the choices you made?

2. What choice has had the greatest effect on your life?

Searching the Scriptures

All the tribes of Israel had gathered in the Valley of Shechem to present themselves before God and to hear Joshua's final words (Joshua 24:1). First, they heard him remind them of their glorious history and of God's rich blessings to them. Abraham, the man they revered so much, had come from a family of idolaters; and it was only the sovereign grace of God that took him from the land of Babylon, brought him into the land of Canaan, and gave him the miracle child, Isaac (vv. 2, 3).

God had plagued Egypt and delivered Israel from the oppression and bondage of that evil nation (vv. 4–7). He had exercised His omnipotence in their behalf, and they were all too prone to forget it. Had not the Lord Himself defeated the Amorites and the Moabites when they had tried to bar the passage of the Children of Israel to the Land of Promise (vv. 8, 9)? God had turned the cursings of Balaam into blessings, and no enemy was able to close his hand on Israel (vv. 10–12). With a mighty miracle God's people crossed over the Jordan. They first overwhelmed Jericho, and then they defeated with precision the Amorites, the Perizzites, the Canaanites, the Hittites, the Girgashites, the Hivites, and the Jebusites.

"I have given you a land for which ye did not labour, and cities which ye built not, and ye dwell in them; of the vineyards and olive-yards which ye planted not do ye eat" (v. 13), the Lord reminded them. God had exercised His omnipotence on Israel's behalf, and His blessings had flowed like unhindered water from the fountainhead. Had the people learned any lasting lessons from the history of God's dealings with them? They certainly should have!

3. Which event in Israel's history from the Exodus to the Conquest impresses you most about God's power?

4. Which event in Israel's history from the Exodus to the Conquest impresses you most about God's grace?

5. Which event in your own life most impresses you with God's power? Why?

6. Which event in your own life most impresses you with God's grace? Why?

As long as the Israelites remembered God's works, "they sang his praise"; but as soon as they "forgat his works," they "lusted exceedingly in the wilderness, and tempted God in the desert" (Psalm 106:12–14).

That was the danger Joshua feared might overtake God's people again. He therefore exhorted Israel to look to the past and to live in the light of God's gracious and marvelous ministry in their behalf. "Now therefore fear the LORD, and serve him in sincerity and in truth: and put away the gods which your fathers served on the other side of the flood, and in Egypt; and serve ye the LORD" (Joshua 24:14).

7. What does it mean to fear the Lord?

8. How might fearing the Lord affect a believer's life?

9. What does it mean to serve the Lord "in sincerity and in truth"?

As a good leader, Joshua let the people know where he stood regarding the Lord: "As for me and my house, we will serve the LORD" (v. 15), he announced. He had always served the Lord, and old age would not keep him from serving the Lord. His consistent love for the Lord and obedience to His commands set an example for the rest of the nation.

His exhortation met with an instantaneous response in the hearts of the Israelites. They exclaimed, "God forbid that we should forsake the LORD" (v. 16).

"Ye cannot serve the LORD," Joshua responded, "for he is an holy God; he is a jealous God; he will not forgive your transgressions nor your sins" (v. 19).

Joshua knew the Israelites well. He understood how prone they were to wander from the Lord. He knew, too, that the Lord was holy and would not wink at His people's sins.

10. Read Joshua 24:20. What could the Israelites expect if they wandered away from the Lord?

11. What do you see as the most painful consequence of wandering away from the Lord today?

12. Why is this consequence so painful?

Having received Joshua's earnest warning, the Israelites renewed their dedication to the Lord and insisted that they desired above all else to serve Him. They said, "Nay; but we will serve the LORD" (v. 21).

Joshua responded, "Ye are witnesses against yourselves that ye have chosen you the LORD, to serve him" (v. 22). With these words, Joshua informed the Israelites that they were entering into a covenant agreement with the Lord. They were pledging themselves to honor and obey the Lord.

Understanding that they were promising their allegiance to the Lord, the people affirmed, "We are witnesses" (v. 22).

13. What evidence of a covenant with the Lord did Joshua demand (Joshua 24:23)?

14. What false gods vie for the allegiance a Christian owes to God alone?

Joshua 24:23 admonishes, "Incline your heart unto the LORD God of Israel." Intentions without a heart inclined toward God are empty and merely lip service. Christ condemned the scribes and Pharisees of His day for living by performance rather than by heart.

15. How does a person incline his or her heart toward God?

Joshua wrote the people's covenant "in the book of the law of God, and took a great stone, and set it up there under an oak, that was by the sanctuary of the LORD. And Joshua said unto all the people, Behold, this stone shall be a witness unto us; for it hath heard all the words of the LORD which he spake unto us: it shall be therefore a witness unto you, lest ye deny your God" (vv. 26, 27).

In the problems, conflicts, and temptations of the days to come, it would be of considerable help to the Israelites to look back to that significant hour of serious dedication to the Lord. It would help hold them fast to remember that they had made a promise to the Lord and that the matter of obedience to Him under all circumstances was a settled issue. When the temptation to waver assailed them, they could look to the rock that bore testimony that they were committed to the Lord; and they would be encouraged to stand firm. That stone of witness was a valuable reminder to each of them.

The Puritans evidently recognized the value of a definite, recorded dedication of life, for it was common among them to put in written form their commitment to Christ. They would write out a statement of their surrender to Christ, affix the date to it, and keep it in their possession as a perpetual reminder that they were not their own but servants of Jesus Christ.

The book of Joshua ends with a brief report of Joshua's death and burial. It also reports the burial of Joseph's bones and the death and burial of Aaron's son Eleazar. Great men of God, like all people, die, but their lives impact eternity.

Making It Personal

16. How well is your heart inclined toward God? Use the scale

below to indicate the inclination of your heart toward God. Draw an arrow from the dot to the point on the scale that best represents your heart's inclination toward God.

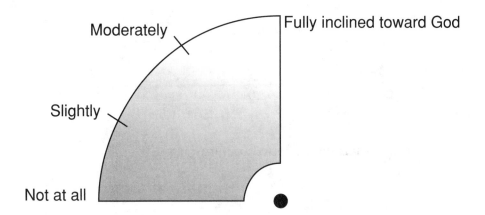

17. What is pulling your heart away from full inclination toward God? Write your answers next to the "Not at all" portion of the scale.

18. What can you do to increase the inclination of your heart toward God?

19. What two or three statements of allegiance to the Lord would you be willing to sign that would represent an increase in the inclination of your heart toward the Lord?

Joshua and the Children of Israel who accompanied him into the Promised Land were certainly changed by the adventure. Knowing

God's character and trusting Him formed the basis for that change.

20. What have you learned about the nature of God through this study?

21. How has this study affected your trust in God?